Monster SATs

Key Stage 1 English

Practice Papers

TEACHER BOOK

12x English Tests: Reading and
Grammar, Punctuation & Spelling

Contents

National curriculum practice tests

Test 1

Key Stage 1

English grammar, punctuation and spelling
Paper 1: spelling

Our Lady of Lourdes Catholic Primary School
Wesley Road
Hillside
London
NW10 8PP
Tel: 020 8961 5037

First name	
Middle name	
Last name	

Total Marks	/ 20

Spelling

P. They will _____ for the bus to arrive.

1. The _____ leaves fell from the tree. ○

2. The boy tried to _____ the ball. ○

3. I could not _____ what you said. ○

4. The time on the _____ was wrong. ○

5. I mended the hole in my _____. ○

6. Last Saturday was a _____ day. ○

7. I eat breakfast early each _____. ○

8. _____ bags were stored in the locker. ○

9. Her _____ went on holiday to Spain. ○

10. Jack was ordered to clean his _____. ○

11. The story was about an angry _____ . ○

12. The plate _____ onto the floor. ○

13. The train arrived at the _____ . ○

14. The girl _____ ate her ice-cream. ○

15. He took a _____ with him to the beach. ○

16. The pupils tried hard to _____ the test. ○

17. The secretary _____ to the letter. ○

18. I have an appointment at the _____ . ○

19. It was _____ for the teacher to be early. ○

20. The _____ was made of bricks. ○

Teacher Sheet

Test 1

Please refer to the spelling script on page 121.

Each spelling is in bold.

P.   They will **wait** for the bus to arrive.

1.   The **green** leaves fell from the tree.

2.   The boy tried to **catch** the ball.

3.   I could not **hear** what you said.

4.   The time on the **watch** was wrong.

5.   I mended the hole in my **jumper**.

6.   Last Saturday was a **warm** day.

7.   I eat breakfast early each **morning**.

8.   **Their** bags were stored in the locker.

9.   Her **family** went on holiday to Spain.

10.   Jack was ordered to clean his **bedroom**.

11.   The story was about an angry **giant**.

12.   The plate **dropped** onto the floor.

13.   The train arrived at the **station**.

14.   The girl **happily** ate her ice-cream.

15.   He took a **towel** with him to the beach.

16.   The pupils tried hard to **complete** the test.

17.   The secretary **replied** to the letter.

18.   I have an appointment at the **hospital**.

19.   It was **usual** for the teacher to be early.

20.   The **chimney** was made of bricks.

National curriculum practice tests

Test 2

Key Stage 1

English grammar, punctuation and spelling

Paper 1: spelling

First name	
Middle name	
Last name	

Total Marks	**/ 20**

Spelling

P. The _____ is closed on Sunday.

_____

1. I went swimming in the _____. ○

2. The girls ran quickly during the _____. ○

3. The building is the largest in the _____. ○

4. I _____ complete my homework. ○

5. I have to sharpen my _____. ○

6. I stood in the _____ of the group. ○

7. The school will be closed on _____. ○

8. The search for the keys was _____. ○

9. I have some loose _____ in my pocket. ○

10. There was a loud _____ at the door. ○

11. The weather was hot in _____. ○

12. I made two _____ of the document. ○

13. My _____ is a nurse. ○

14. I opened my _____ widely. ○

15. This bread is _____ than that one. ○

16. The postman _____ the letters. ○

17. The car drove through the _____. ○

18. She _____ the dog on the head. ○

19. The little child was _____ of the dark. ○

20. I know all the letters of the _____. ○

Teacher Sheet

Test 2

Please refer to the spelling script on page 121.

Each spelling is in bold.

P.   The **bank** is closed on Sunday.

1.   I went swimming in the **sea**.

2.   The girls ran quickly during the **race**.

3.   The building is the largest in the **world**.

4.   I **always** complete my homework.

5.   I have to sharpen my **pencil**.

6.   I stood in the **middle** of the group.

7.   The school will be closed on **Wednesday**.

8.   The search for the keys was **hopeless**.

9.   I have some loose **change** in my pocket.

10. There was a loud **knock** at the door.

11. The weather was hot in **July**.

12. I made two **copies** of the document.

13. My **sister** is a nurse.

14. I opened my **mouth** widely.

15. This bread is **fresher** than that one.

16. The postman **carries** the letters.

17. The car drove through the **tunnel**.

18. She **patted** the dog on the head.

19. The little child was **scared** of the dark.

20. I know all the letters of the **alphabet**.

National curriculum practice tests

Test 3

Key Stage 1

English grammar, punctuation and spelling
Paper 1: spelling

First name	
Middle name	
Last name	

Total Marks	/ 20

Spelling

P. I am not feeling _____ today.

_____

1. The boy _____ a medal. ◯

2. There are many types of _____. ◯

3. No-one could hear a _____ in the cave. ◯

4. Please be _____ with the cups. ◯

5. The novel was _____ a long time ago. ◯

6. My flowers are _____ than yours. ◯

7. There was _____ in the box. ◯

8. I forgot to take my football _____. ◯

9. The _____ kitten slept in its basket. ◯

10. The _____ was below the mountain. ◯

11. We travelled over the _____. ◯

12. I hurt my _____ in the playground. ◯

13. The singer was _____ a tune. ◯

14. The _____ on the bicycle was broken. ◯

15. I will _____ the birthday present. ◯

16. The plants grew in the _____. ◯

17. The _____ stole the diamond. ◯

18. The girl was from a small _____. ◯

19. The _____ of France is Paris. ◯

20. We saw a _____ at the zoo. ◯

Teacher Sheet

Test 3

Please refer to the spelling script on page 121.

Each spelling is in bold.

P.   I am not feeling **well** today.

1.   The boy **won** a medal.

2.   There are many types of **rocks**.

3.   No-one could hear a **sound** in the cave.

4.   Please be **careful** with the cups.

5.   The novel was **written** a long time ago.

6.   My flowers are **nicer** than yours.

7.   There was **nothing** in the box.

8.   I forgot to take my football **kit**.

9.   The **little** kitten slept in its basket.

10.   The **valley** was below the mountain.

11.   We travelled over the **bridge**.

12.   I hurt my **knee** in the playground.

13.   The singer was **humming** a tune.

14.   The **pedal** on the bicycle was broken.

15.   I will **wrap** the birthday present.

16.   The plants grew in the **soil**.

17.   The **thief** stole the diamond.

18.   The girl was from a small **village**.

19.   The **capital** of France is Paris.

20.   We saw a **dolphin** at the zoo.

National curriculum practice tests

Test 4

Key Stage 1

English grammar, punctuation and spelling

Paper 1: spelling

First name	
Middle name	
Last name	

Total Marks	/ 20

Spelling

P. I _____ money for my train ticket.

_____

1. I _____ in a large town. ◯

2. The tiny _____ wriggled in the soil. ◯

3. Last _____ I went to Spain. ◯

4. My _____ is a teacher. ◯

5. I _____ home from school. ◯

6. The _____ on the car was punctured. ◯

7. A _____ tree fell on the road. ◯

8. The heavy _____ were unpacked. ◯

9. The busy _____ was very noisy. ◯

10. The _____ stood in the field. ◯

11. I _____ I will go to the park. ◯

12. A strange _____ lived in the cave. ◯

13. The baby was _____ loudly. ◯

14. The girl _____ a letter to her friend. ◯

15. Play the _____ again. ◯

16. The child _____ out the candles. ◯

17. The chest was filled with _____. ◯

18. I put on my _____ as it was cold. ◯

19. The fireman tried to _____ the cat. ◯

20. The _____ fought bravely. ◯

Teacher Sheet

Test 4

Please refer to the spelling script on page 121.

Each spelling is in bold.

P.   I **have** money for my train ticket.

1.   I **live** in a large town.

2.   The tiny **worm** wriggled in the soil.

3.   Last **summer** I went to Spain.

4.   My **brother** is a teacher.

5.   I **walked** home from school.

6.   The **wheel** on the car was punctured.

7.   A **huge** tree fell on the road.

8.   The heavy **boxes** were unpacked.

9.   The busy **city** was very noisy.

10.   The **donkey** stood in the field.

11.   I **think** I will go to the park.

12.   A strange **animal** lived in the cave.

13.   The baby was **crying** loudly.

14.   The girl **wrote** a letter to her friend.

15.   Play the **tune** again.

16.   The child **blew** out the candles.

17.   The chest was filled with **treasure**.

18.   I put on my **jacket** as it was cold.

19.   The fireman tried to **rescue** the cat.

20.   The **knight** fought bravely.

National curriculum practice tests

Test 1

Key Stage 1

English grammar, punctuation and spelling

Paper 2: questions

First name	
Middle name	
Last name	

Total Marks	/ 20

Practice questions

a   Tick the word that completes the sentence.

They were _____ at the photographs.

Tick **one**.

looked	☐
looking	☐
look	☐
looks	☐

b   Circle the **adjective** in the sentence below.

The   bright   star   shone   in   the   sky.

1 Circle the **two** verbs in the sentence below.

The   teacher   shouted   loudly   and   sat   down.

1 mark

2 Write the missing punctuation mark to complete the sentence below.

How   often   do   you   go   to   the   library

1 mark

3 What type of word is underlined in the sentence below?

The pupils in the class were very <u>noisy</u>.

Tick **one**.

a noun ☐

a verb ☐

an adjective ☐

an adverb ☐

1 mark

4 Tick the correct word to complete the sentence below.

I revise for my exams _____ *I want to do well.*

Tick one.

but ☐

or ☐

that ☐

because ☐

○ 1 mark

5 Add a prefix to the word <u>happy</u> to complete the sentence below.

The boy was _____<u>happy</u> *with his present.*

○ 1 mark

6 Circle the **three** nouns in the sentence below.

Lions usually hunt for food during the night.

○ 1 mark

7 Read the sentences below.

> ## Swimming safety
>
> Take a shower before entering the pool.
>
> Use goggles to protect your eyes.
>
> Be respectful to others in the pool.

Tick the word that best describes these sentences.

Tick **one**.

statements ☐

questions ☐

commands ☐

exclamations ☐

1 mark

8 Why do the underlined words start with a **capital letter**?

My sister is called <u>Lucy</u> and her favourite book is <u>Treasure Island</u>.

_____

_____

1 mark

9 What is the function of the sentence below?

What a clever person you are

Tick **one**.

a statement ☐

a question ☐

a command ☐

an exclamation ☐

1 mark

10 Tick the correct word to complete the sentence below.

Is it Monday _____ Tuesday today?

Tick **one**.

or ☐

and ☐

but ☐

if ☐

1 mark

11 Tick to show whether each sentence is in the **past tense** or the **present tense**.

Sentence	Past tense	Present tense
Ben slowly walked home.		
Ben went into the shop.		
Ben looks at the magazines.		

○

1 mark

12 Add one **comma** to the sentence below in the correct place.

There   are   pens   pencils   and   rulers   on   the   table.

○

1 mark

13 Add a **suffix** to the word <u>sharp</u> to complete the sentence below.

I will <u>sharp   </u> the pencils in the box.

○

1 mark

14 What type of sentence is below?

Yesterday, I made a carrot cake.

Tick **one**.

a statement ☐

a question ☐

a command ☐

an exclamation ☐

1 mark

15 Circle the correct verbs so that the sentence is in the **past tense**.

The tickets | are | were | *bought at the station*

1 mark

and we | caught | catch | *the train.*

16 Ben and Sidrah are learning about birds.

Write a question they could ask their teacher in the speech bubble.

Remember to use correct punctuation.

2 marks

17 Circle the **adverb** in the sentence below.

Silently, he crept up the stairs.

1 mark

18 Look at where the arrow is pointing.

Lucy went to the shop James stayed at home.

Which punctuation mark is missing?

Tick **one**.

exclamation mark ☐

question mark ☐

apostrophe ☐

full stop ☐

1 mark

19 Which sentence uses an **apostrophe** correctly?

Tick **one**.

Jack's apples were placed into the baskets. ☐

Jacks apple's were placed into the baskets. ☐

Jacks apples were placed into the baskets'. ☐

Jacks' apples were placed into the baskets. ☐

1 mark

National curriculum practice tests

Test 2

Key Stage 1

English grammar, punctuation and spelling
Paper 2: questions

First name	
Middle name	
Last name	

Total Marks	/ 20

Practice questions

a Write one word on the line below to complete the sentence in the **past tense**.

I _____ to the beach on Saturday.

b Write the missing punctuation mark to complete the sentence below.

How   old   are   you

1 Rearrange the words below to make it a sentence.

Use only the given words.

sister   my   library   the   visited

_____

1 mark

2 Circle the **verbs** in the sentence below.

A   tree   fell   on   the   road   and   stopped   the   traffic.

1 mark

3 Circle the **two** nouns in the sentence below.

The   school   will   be   closed   on   Friday.

◯

1 mark

4 Tick the correct word to complete the sentence below.

The girl was only six years old _____ she sang in the choir.

Tick **one**.

because ☐

or ☐

that ☐

when ☐

◯

1 mark

5 Why do the underlined words start with a **capital letter**?

Next <u>Friday</u>, we are going to visit my friend <u>James</u> in <u>Manchester</u>.

_____

_____

◯

1 mark

6 Tick the sentence that is a **statement**.

Tick **one**.

Where is your homework?   ☐

Place the newspapers in the rubbish bin.   ☐

Lucy cleaned her bedroom yesterday.   ☐

What wonderful news!   ☐

◯

1 mark

7 Write the words <u>would not</u> as one word, using an **apostrophe**.

The glasses _____ fit into the cupboard.

◯
1 mark

8 Which sentence is a **command**?

Tick **one**.

Chop the carrots and onions carefully. ☐

Have you added milk to the tea? ☐

I am not sure where the museum is. ☐

What an exciting day! ☐

◯
1 mark

9 Jack wants to know more about bread. His father is a baker.

Write a question he could ask his father in the speech bubble.

Remember to use correct punctuation.

2 marks

10 Write **s** or **es** to make each word a plural.

box_____

lesson_____

watch_____

1 mark

11 The verbs in boxes are in the present tense.
Write these verbs in the **past tense**.

One has been done for you.

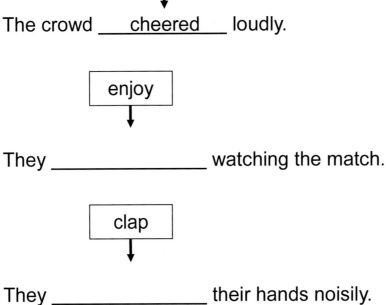

| cheers |

The crowd ____cheered____ loudly.

| enjoy |

They _____ watching the match.

| clap |

They _____ their hands noisily.

2 marks

12 What type of word is <u>plain</u> in the sentence below?

The girl wore a plain black dress.

Tick **one**.

an adverb ☐

an adjective ☐

a verb ☐

a noun ☐

1 mark

13 Tick to show whether each sentence is in the **past tense** or the **present tense**.

Sentence	Past tense	Present tense
The book is over there.		
The shelves are dusty.		
I lifted the book off the shelf.		

1 mark

14 Tick the sentence that is correct.

Tick **one**.

James buy a coat and wore it to school. ☐

James bought a coat and wear it to school. ☐

James buy a coat and worn it to school. ☐

James bought a coat and wore it to school. ☐

1 mark

15 Circle the **full stops** that are in the wrong places.

One has been done for you.

The bus. will leave the station on. Wednesday

morning. James will collect. you and your friend.

1 mark

16 Tick one box to show where a **comma** should go in the sentence below.

Tick **one**.

For my breakfast I had juice tea and a slice of toast.

⬆   ⬆   ⬆   ⬆

☐   ☐   ☐   ☐

1 mark

17 What type of word is underlined in the sentence below?

James <u>carefully</u> folded his clothes.

Tick **one**.

an adjective ☐

an adverb ☐

a noun ☐

a verb ☐

○

1 mark

18 Which punctuation mark completes the sentence below?

What a delicious meal you have cooked

Tick **one**.

apostrophe ☐

exclamation mark ☐

question mark ☐

comma ☐

○

1 mark

National curriculum practice tests

Test 3

Key Stage 1

English grammar, punctuation and spelling
Paper 2: questions

First name	
Middle name	
Last name	

Total Marks	/ 20

Practice questions

a   Circle the adjective in the sentence below.

My   helpful   neighbour   carried   my   bags.

b   Tick the word that completes the sentence.

The cat was _____ the mouse.

Tick one.

chased	☐
chasing	☐
chase	☐
chases	☐

1 What type of sentence is below?

Place your empty cans in the recycling bin.

Tick **one**.

a statement ☐

a question ☐

a command ☐

an exclamation ☐

1 mark

2 Circle the **two** verbs in the sentence below.

The girl stood by the window and looked outside.

1 mark

3 Add a **suffix** to the word <u>slow</u> to complete the sentence below.

I slow_____ crossed the road.

1 mark

4 Circle the **adverb** in the sentence below.

My sister kindly offered to bake a cake.

◯
1 mark

5 Tick the correct word to complete the sentence below.

_____ *you do your homework, you can go outside.*

Tick one.

and ☐

so ☐

but ☐

if ☐

◯
1 mark

6 Write the words <u>will</u> <u>not</u> as one word, using an **apostrophe**.

I _____ go to the party.

○
1 mark

7 Write the missing punctuation mark to complete the sentence below.

What is the capital of England

○
1 mark

8 Circle the **three** nouns in the sentence below.

My cousin is called Lucy and she lives in

Italy.

○
1 mark

9 Circle the **full stops** that are in the wrong places.
One has been done for you.

My favourite football team is called. Norwich

United. I go to see them play each. Saturday

with my dad.

1 mark

10 The verbs in boxes are in the present tense.
Write these verbs in the **past tense**.
One has been done for you.

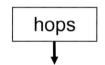

The rabbit __hopped__ around the field.

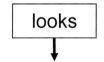

It _____ for some food to eat.

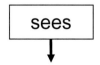

It finally _____ a carrot in the field.

2 marks

11 Tick the sentence that is a **statement**.

Tick **one**.

How lucky you are! ☐

Listen carefully to the teacher. ☐

Are you going to the birthday party? ☐

The rain fell heavily during the night. ☐

1 mark

12 Add one comma to the sentence below in the correct place.

1 mark

The pizza has mushrooms onions and peppers.

13 Tick to show whether each sentence is in the **past tense** or the **present tense**.

Sentence	Past tense	Present tense
I went to my local park on Monday.		
I watch the ducks on the pond.		
I enjoy going to the park each day.		

1 mark

14 What type of word is underlined in the sentence below?

The <u>lonely</u> moon was glowing in the sky.

Tick **one**.

a noun ☐

a verb ☐

an adjective ☐

an adverb ☐

1 mark

15 Why do the underlined words start with a **capital letter**?

I go to the beach with my friend <u>James</u> during <u>August</u>.

_____

_____

◯

1 mark

16 Tick the sentence that is correct.

Tick one.

Jack ate his dinner and drink his glass of milk. ☐

Jack eats his dinner and drank his glass of milk. ☐

Jack ate his dinner and drinks his glass of milk. ☐

Jack ate his dinner and drank his glass of milk. ☐

◯

1 mark

17 Draw lines to match the groups of words that have the same meaning.

One has been done for you.

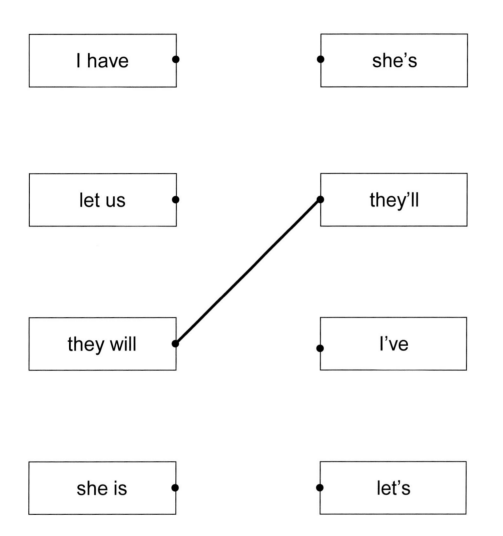

1 mark

18 Sam wants to know more about tractors. His neighbour is a farmer.

Write a question he could ask his neighbour in the speech bubble.

Remember to use correct punctuation.

2 marks

National curriculum practice tests

Test 4

Key Stage 1

English grammar, punctuation and spelling
Paper 2: questions

First name	
Middle name	
Last name	

Total Marks	/ 20

Practice questions

a Write the missing punctuation mark to complete the sentence below.

Where   are   you   going

b Write one word on the line below to complete the sentence in the **past tense**.

The birds _____ the seeds.

1 Circle the **two** nouns in the sentence below.

The large lake was below the mountain.

◯
1 mark

2 Which sentence is a **command**?

Tick **one**.

Where are your shoes? ☐

The old man fell asleep. ☐

The museum is open today. ☐

Close the door quietly. ☐

◯
1 mark

3 Why do the underlined words start with a **capital letter**?

The National Bank is open every day apart from Saturday and Sunday.

_____

_____

◯
1 mark

4 Circle the **two** verbs in the sentence below.

The horse jumped over the fence and crossed the field.

◯
1 mark

5 What type of word is <u>calm</u> in the sentence below?

The boat sailed on the calm sea.

Tick **one**.

an adverb ☐

an adjective ☐

a verb ☐

a noun ☐

◯
1 mark

6 Rearrange the words below to make it a sentence.

Use only the given words.

friend   *scored*   *goal*   *a*   *my*

_____

1 mark

7 Tick the correct word to complete the sentence below.

I was ill _____ *I did not go to the doctor.*

Tick one.

or ☐

so ☐

but ☐

if ☐

1 mark

8 Write the missing punctuation mark to complete the sentence below.

How high is the mountain

○
1 mark

9 Tick the sentence that is correct.

Tick one.

Lucy cleans the table and washed the dishes. ☐

Lucy cleaned the table and washed the dishes. ☐

Lucy clean the table and washes the dishes. ☐

Lucy cleans the table and wash the dishes. ☐

○
1 mark

10 What is the function of the sentence below?

What an amazing friend you are

Tick one.

a statement ☐

a question ☐

a command ☐

an exclamation ☐

1 mark

11 Add **one** comma to the sentence below in the correct place.

We saw ducks rabbits and birds at the park.

1 mark

12 Circle the **adverb** in the sentence below.

The soldier bravely fought during the battle.

1 mark

13 Tick to show whether each sentence is in the **past tense** or the **present tense**.

Sentence	Past tense	Present tense
The boy whistled loudly.		
This chair is broken.		
I washed the car today.		

1 mark

14 Tick the correct word to complete the sentence below.

I think _____ *the bus will be arriving soon.*

Tick **one**.

when	☐
if	☐
that	☐
because	☐

1 mark

15 What type of sentence is below?

The weather is very hot in France.

Tick **one**.

a statement ☐

a question ☐

a command ☐

an exclamation ☐

1 mark

16 Look at where the arrow is pointing.

Lucy made a cake Ben made a pizza.

↑

Which punctuation mark is missing?

Tick **one**.

exclamation mark ☐

question mark ☐

apostrophe ☐

full stop ☐

1 mark

17 Sidrah wants to know more about plants.

Her friend is a gardener.

Write a question Sidrah could ask her friend in the speech bubble.

Remember to use correct punctuation.

○

2 marks

18 Write **s** or **es** to make each word a plural.

echo_____

pencil_____

potato_____

○

1 mark

19 Draw lines to match the groups of words that have the same meaning.

One has been done for you.

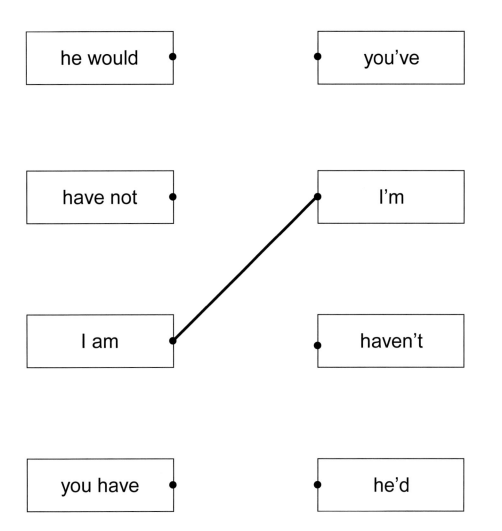

○
1 mark

National curriculum practice tests

Key Stage 1

Test 1

English reading

Paper 1: reading prompt and answer booklet

First name	
Middle name	
Last name	

Total Marks	/ 20

Useful words

quite

grown-up

Bed in Summer

~ Robert Louis Stevenson

In Winter I get up at night
And dress by yellow candle light.
In Summer, quite the other way,
I have to go to bed by day.

I have to go to bed and see
The birds still hopping on the tree,
Or hear the grown-up people's feet
Still going past me in the street.

And does it not seem hard to you,
When all the sky is clear and blue,
And I should like so much to play,
To have to go to bed by day?

Practice questions

a Which two seasons are mentioned in the poem?

_____ and _____

b What colour is the candle light?

_____

1 (a) What does the speaker see when in bed?

_____

(b) What does the speaker hear when in bed?

_____ ◯

2 What does the speaker want to do instead of going to bed?

_____ ◯

3 **Find** and **copy** two words which describe the sky.

1. _____

2. _____ ◯

4   *In Summer, quite the other way*

What does this line mean?

_____

_____

◯

1 mark

5   *And does it not seem hard to you...*

Who is the speaker talking to?
Tick **one**.

The grown-ups ☐   The birds ☐

The sky ☐   The reader ☐

◯

1 mark

6   Why might it seem to the speaker that they sleep during the day in Summer?

_____

_____

◯

1 mark

Useful words

masts

sigh

splendid

The Fir Tree - Hans Christian Andersen

Out in the woods stood a little Fir Tree.

He was in a wonderful place. The sun could shine on him. There was enough fresh air. Around him grew many large trees, both fir trees and pines.

However, the little Fir Tree wanted very much to be a grown-up.

Practice question

a What does the little Fir Tree want?

Tick **one**.

To have the sun shine on him. ☐   To have enough fresh air. ☐

To be a grown-up. ☐   To be a pine tree. ☐

69

The Fir Tree did not think about the warm sun or of the fresh air. He did not care about the little children who ran and laughed when they were looking for wild strawberries and raspberries.

Often they came with a whole jug full of juice, or had their strawberries strung on a straw, and sat down near the little Fir Tree and said, "Oh, what a nice little tree!" This was what the Fir Tree could not bear to hear.

---

7 Give **two** things that the Fir Tree did not think about.

1. _____

2. _____

○
1 mark

8 *This was what the Fir Tree could not bear to hear.*

Explain the meaning of this sentence.

_____

_____

○
1 mark

In autumn the wood-cutters always came and chopped down some of the largest trees.

This happened every year and the young Fir Tree, which was now quite well grown, trembled at the sight. The large trees would fall to the earth with a loud noise and their branches were cut off. The trees looked bare and were so long and thin that you would hardly know them for trees. They were then placed on carts and horses dragged them out of the wood.

Where did they go? What became of them?

9 What happened to some of the largest trees in autumn?

_____

1 mark

10 *trembled at the sight*

What does this reveal how the Fir Tree feels?
Tick **one**.

It is afraid. ☐   It is happy. ☐

It is angry. ☐   It is annoyed. ☐

1 mark

In spring, when the Swallow and the Stork came, the Fir Tree asked them, "Do you know where the trees have been taken to? Have you not met them anywhere?"

The Swallow did not know anything about it; but the Stork nodded his head and said, "Yes; I know where they go. I met many new ships as I was flying from Egypt. On the ships were large wooden masts and I think they were made from the fir trees."

11 When did the Swallow and Stork visit the Fir Tree?

_____

○

1 mark

12 Which country was the Stork flying from when it saw the ships?

_____

○

1 mark

13 What did the Stork think had happened to the trees?

_____

_____

○

1 mark

"Oh, were I old enough to fly across the sea! How does the sea really look and what is it like?"

"Aye, that takes too long to tell," said the Stork. "Enjoy your youth!"

Though the Fir Tree did not understand.

- -

Over the years, the Fir Tree grew and grew and was green both winter and summer. One December, he was one of the first trees to be cut down. The axe struck deep into the trunk and the Fir Tree fell to the earth with a sigh.

---

14 Find and copy one word that means *being young*.

_____

1 mark

15 *fell to the earth with a sigh*

Why do you think the Fir tree fell *with a sigh*?
Tick **one**.

It was frightened about being cut down. ☐

It was sad to be cut down. ☐

It was anxious about being cut down. ☐

It was happy to be cut down. ☐

1 mark

Next the Fir Tree found himself in a courtyard with other trees. He heard an old man say, "That one is splendid! We don't want the others." Then two servants came and carried the Fir Tree into a large, wonderful room.

In the room, pictures were hanging on the walls and there were large chairs and tables, which were full of picture-books and toys.

---

16 *That one is splendid!*

What does the word *splendid* mean in this sentence?
Tick **one**.

terrible   strange

wonderful ☐   old ☐

1 mark

17 What objects were on the chairs and tables?

_____

1 mark

The Fir Tree was placed upright in a box filled with sand. Oh, how the Tree shivered!

As the moon shone, the servants placed different objects on the tree. On one branch there hung little nets cut out of coloured paper. Each net was filled with plums, apples and walnuts. There were also more than a hundred little red, gold and silver pieces of paper placed into the branches. The Fir Tree was overcome with joy.

18 Find and copy one word which shows the tree is standing straight up.

_____

1 mark

19 How can you tell that it was late when the servants placed objects on the tree?

_____

_____

1 mark

20 How does the Fir Tree feel at the end of the story?

sad ☐ worried ☐

annoyed ☐ happy ☐

○
1 mark

National curriculum practice tests

Test 2

Key Stage 1

English reading

Paper 1: reading prompt and answer booklet

First name	
Middle name	
Last name	

Total Marks	/ 20

Useful words

planet

orbits

explosive

The Sun

The Sun is our nearest star. Without the Sun there would be no daylight and our planet would simply be a dark, frozen world, with no water and no life.

Practice question

a What is the Sun?

Tick **one**.

A planet ☐   A star ☐

A world ☐   A life ☐

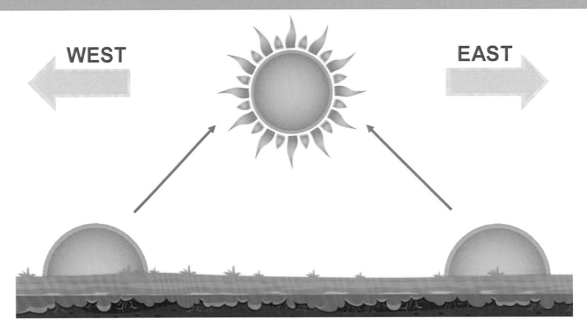

WEST

EAST

From Earth, the Sun looks like it moves across the sky in the day and appears to disappear at night. This is because the Earth is spinning towards the east.

The Earth orbits around the Sun. It takes one year to go around the Sun one complete time. The Earth spins around an axis. It means that the Sun seems to rise in the east in the morning and climb higher and higher in the sky towards midday. In the afternoon the Sun then seems to move lower in the sky before setting in the west.

1 In which direction does the Earth spin towards?

_____

1 mark

2 *The Earth orbits around the Sun.*

How long does this take?

one month ☐   one day ☐

one week ☐   one year ☐

1 mark

80

Although the Sun seems small when seen at sunrise or sunset, this is only because the Sun is about 150 million km away from us.

At this distance, it takes about eight minutes for sunlight to reach the Earth – even when it is travelling at about 300,000 km per second.

This means that we see the Sun set eight minutes after the event has actually taken place.

3 How long does it take for sunlight to reach the Earth?

_____

1 mark

4 How many miles away from the Earth is the Sun?

_____

1 mark

5 During which points of the day, does the Sun seem small? List **two**.

1. _____

2. _____

1 mark

The Sun provides us with light and heat. It also gives out dangerous ultra-violet light which can cause sunburn.

The Sun becomes more active every 11 years. At such times, the number of dark sunspots on its surface increases. At the peak of the sunspot cycle, there are many more explosive solar storms.

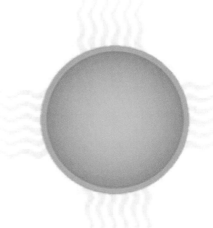

---

6   What type of light can cause sunburn?

_____

○

1 mark

7   What happens at the peak of the sunspot cycle?

_____

_____

○

1 mark

8   Give **two** things that the Sun provides us with.

1. _____

2. _____

○

1 mark

82

Useful words

urgently

impatient

grumbling

The Mole had been working very hard all morning spring-cleaning his little home.

First with brooms, then with dusters; then on ladders and steps and chairs, with a brush and a bucket of whitewash. All until he had dust in his throat and eyes and splashes of whitewash all over his black fur. He had an aching back and arms and felt weak.

Spring was in the air above and in the earth below and around him. He could sense it even in his dark, little house.

---

9 Where is the Mole at the beginning of the story?

_____

○ 1 mark

10 What season is it?

_____

○ 1 mark

11 How did the Mole feel after cleaning his home?

bored ☐   angry ☐

tired ☐   cheerful ☐

○ 1 mark

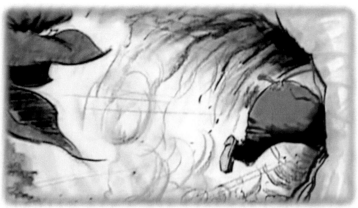

It was no wonder, then, that he suddenly flung down his brush on the floor, said `Bother!' and `Hang spring-cleaning!' He bolted out of the house without even waiting to put on his coat.

Something up above was calling him urgently. He therefore hurried to the steep, little tunnel which was owned by animals whose homes were nearer to the sun and air.

12 *He bolted out of the house...*

What does the word *bolted* mean in this sentence?

Tick **one**.

to move quickly ☐   to shout loudly ☐

to walk slowly ☐   to jump noisily ☐

1 mark

13 **Find** and **copy two** words that describe the tunnel.

1. _____

2. _____

1 mark

So he scraped and scratched and scrabbled and scrooged. Then he scrooged again and scrabbled and scratched and scraped, working busily with his little paws and muttering to himself, `Up we go! Up we go!'.

Until at last, pop! His snout came out into the sunlight and he found himself rolling in the grass of a great meadow.

---

14 What sound was made when the Mole's snout came out of the tunnel?

_____

○

1 mark

15 List **two** actions that the Mole does in order to get out of the tunnel.

1. _____

2. _____

○

1 mark

16 How can you tell that it was daytime when the Mole came out of his tunnel?

_____

○

1 mark

'Hold up!' shouted an old rabbit at the gap. `Sixpence for the honour of passing by the private road!' He was shocked by the impatient Mole, who trotted along the side of the hedge. The Mole laughed at the other rabbits as they peeped hurriedly from their holes to see what the row was about.

`Onion-sauce! Onion-sauce!' the Mole said and vanished before the rabbits could think of what to say.

Then they all started grumbling at each other. However, it was all too late.

---

17 Why did the old rabbit tell the Mole to 'Hold up!'?

_____

1 mark

18 What did the old rabbit want from the Mole?

_____

_____

1 mark

19 **Find** and **copy one** word which has the same meaning as *disappeared*.

_____

1 mark

20 Number the sentences below from 1 to 4 to show the order they happen in the story.

The first one has been done for you.

The Mole made his way through the tunnel. ☐

An old rabbit asked the Mole to stop. ☐

The Mole sat on the grass in a meadow. ☐

The Mole was spring-cleaning his home. 1

1 mark

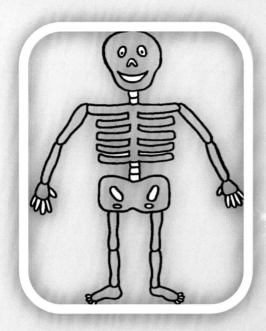

The Skeleton

The Little Lame Prince

Reading booklet

Key stage 1 English reading booklet

THE SKELETON

The skeleton is what gives each person their shape.

Although bones appear very hard, under the surface they are more like sponges, with lots of air. This makes bones very strong, but very light.

The adult human body has 206 bones in the skeleton. These bones are grown together from about 300 bones at birth.

Bones are broken down and remade constantly, just like skin. In fact, all of the bones are slowly replaced until they are new. This happens once every seven years.

The spine, which runs down the middle of the back, allows the body to bend forward, backward, side to side, and rotate to each side.

The spine provides support for the top of the body (everything above the hips), and also protects the spinal cord.

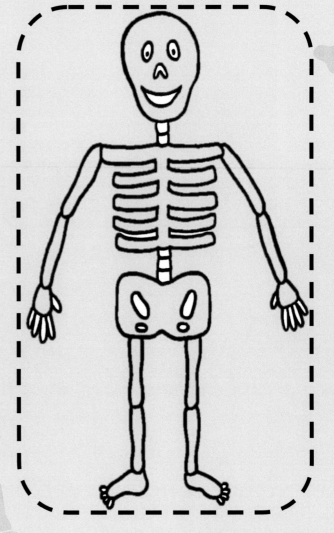

The skull, which contains the brain and protects it, is made up of different bones which grow together during childhood. It has places for the eyes and ears and only has one moving part - the lower jaw bone.

The ribs, which are in your chest, give support for your lungs, heart and upper body muscles. One of the biggest jobs the ribs have is to protect the heart and lungs and also the kidneys.

The insides of some bones contain special material called bone marrow. Bone marrow has lots of cells which make red blood cells. Red blood cells carry oxygen all over the body. Every second, bone marrow produces two million red blood cells.

The best way to look at bones is with a special photo called an X-ray. X-rays help tell doctors where there is a broken bone so they know how to repair it.

The Little Lame Prince

Prince Dolor had never seen anything like it. Despite feeling disappointed, he looked at the cloak curiously. He spread it out on the door, then arranged it on his shoulders. It felt very warm and comfortable but it was so ragged - the most ragged thing that the Prince had ever seen in his life.

"And what use will it be to me?" said he sadly. "I have no need of outdoor clothes, as I never go outside as my legs are too weak. Why was this given to me, I wonder? What in the world am I to do with it? She must be a strange person, this dear godmother of mine."

Nevertheless, because she was his godmother and had given him the cloak, he folded it carefully and put it away. Even though it was ragged, he hid it in a safe corner of his top cupboard, where no-one would look. He did not want anyone to find it, or to laugh at it or at his godmother.

There it lay in the cupboard and he forgot all about it. Being a child and not seeing his godmother again, he almost forgot her. He sometimes thought of her as he did of the angels or fairies that he read of in his books. It seemed as if her visit had been a strange dream during the night.

Of course, there were times when he thought of her, such as early in the morning. Or sometimes he would think of her late in the evening, when the grey night light reminded him of the colour of her hair and her pretty soft clothes.

Above all, he would think of her most when waking in the middle of the night, with the stars peering in at his window or the moonlight shining across his little bed. At those moments he would not have been surprised to see her standing beside his bed, looking at him with those beautiful kind eyes. They seemed to have a comfort in them which was different from anything he had ever known.

However, his godmother never came back and gradually she slipped out of his memory. However he wanted her to return as he had never wanted anything before.

- -

Soon after, Prince Dolor fell ill. One morning, he caught an illness which made him very angry and disagreeable. Even when he was beginning to feel a little better, he was too weak to enjoy anything, but lay all day long on his bed. There he lay alone, very alone.

Now and then a feeling came over him, in which he longed to get up and do something, or go somewhere. He would have liked to be his white kitten and jump down from his room and run away, taking the chance of whatever might happen.

Only one thing was likely to happen; for the kitten, he remembered, had four active legs, while he could no longer use his.

"I wonder what my godmother thought when she looked at my weak legs? I wonder why I can't walk straight and steady like everyone else? It would be nice to move about quickly. Perhaps to fly, like a bird, like that string of birds I saw the other day flying across the sky, one after the other."

These were the passage-birds - the only living creatures that ever crossed the deserted and lonely land where the Prince lived. He had so much interest in them, wondering where they came from and where they were going.

The Prince felt exhausted. He gathered himself up and lay his head upon his hands. As he did so, he felt somebody kiss him at the back of his neck. Turning around, he found that he was resting, not on the pillows on his bed, but on a warm shoulder. It was that of his little old godmother, clothed in grey.

National curriculum practice tests

Test 1

Key Stage 1

English reading
Paper 2: reading answer booklet

First name	
Middle name	
Last name	

Total Marks	/ 20

> **Questions 1-8 are about**
> ***The Skeleton* (pages 90-91)**

(page 90)

1 Complete the sentence below.

The skeleton is what gives each person their _____.

◯
1 mark

(page 90)

2 After how many years are old bones replaced?

_____

◯
1 mark

(page 90)

3 Tick **two** facts about bones.

Bones are ...

Tick **two**.

strong ☐

heavy ☐

square ☐

light ☐

◯
1 mark

(page 90)

4 How many bones are in an adult human body?

_____

○
1 mark

(page 90)

5 *Bones are broken down and remade constantly.*

What does the word *constantly* mean?

Tick one.

changing now and then ☐

breaking slowly ☐

happening all the time ☐

connecting quickly ☐

○
1 mark

(page 90)

6 What does the spine give support to?

Give **two** things.

1. _____

2. _____

○
1 mark

(page 91)

7 What is the function of red blood cells?

_____

_____

○
1 mark

(page 91)

8 Put ticks in the table to show which sentences are **true** and which are **false**.

The information says that...	True	False
The skull has two moving parts.		
Bone marrow produces two million red blood cells every second.		
An X-ray tells doctors where there is a broken bone.		
The ribs give support to your lungs, heart and upper body muscles.		

2 marks

Questions 9-18 are about
The Little Lame Prince (pages 92-94)

(page 92)

9 Who gave the cloak to Prince Dolor?

_____

○
1 mark

(page 92)

10 *he looked at the cloak curiously*

What does this reveal about the Prince's feelings towards the cloak?

_____

_____

○
1 mark

(page 92)

11 Give **two** reasons why the Prince hides the cloak.

1. _____

_____

2. _____

_____

○
2 marks

(page 93)

12 When did the Prince think most about his godmother?

_____

○
1 mark

(page 93)

13 *gradually she slipped out of his memory*

What does this mean?

Tick **one**.

Prince Dolor's godmother fell over. ☐

Prince Dolor remembered his godmother. ☐

Prince Dolor forgot about his godmother. ☐

Prince Dolor had a weak memory. ☐

○
1 mark

(page 93)

14 **Find** and **copy two** words that describe how the Prince felt on the morning when he became ill.

1. _____

2. _____

○
1 mark

(page 93)

15 The Prince longed to get up and do something or go somewhere.

Why did the Prince not do this?

_____

_____

○

1 mark

(page 94)

16 *The Prince felt exhausted.*

What does the word *exhausted* mean?

Tick **one**.

tired ☐

upset ☐

frightened ☐

excited ☐

○

1 mark

(page 94)

17 How do you know the Prince lived in a land where there were not many people?

_____

_____

○

1 mark

(pages 92-94)

18 Look at the whole story.

Number the sentences 1 to 4 to show the order that they happen in the story.

Prince Dolor's godmother visited him again. ☐

Prince Dolor became very ill. ☐

Prince Dolor's godmother gave him a cloak. ☐

Prince Dolor wished he could fly like a bird. ☐

○

1 mark

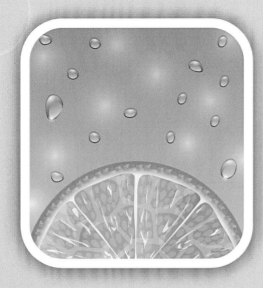

Vitamin C

Oliver Twist

Reading

Key stage 1 English reading booklet

VITAMIN C

Our bodies require many different things to keep us healthy. One group of things we need every day is vitamins.

Vitamins help run many different jobs in our body, from helping to make our food into energy to allowing us to think.

Vitamins are found in lots of foods, but mainly fruits and vegetables. Vitamin C, can be found in citrus fruits like oranges and helps with healing, our immune system and also keeps your teeth healthy.

Vitamin C dissolves (or disappears) in liquid. What does this mean for your body? This means that your body can't hold onto vitamin C for very long when you eat it, so you need to have it every day.

Did you know?

*   Vitamin C can be lost from foods that are cooked, or are stored in water. You should eat fresh fruits and vegetables whenever possible. Also don't store fruits and vegetables in water.

*   Vitamin C helps your brain! It is important in making a special chemical in the brain that helps your brain to function.

*   Vitamin C was the very first vitamin to be man-made and taken as a pill.

*   Vitamin C is sometimes used to treat colds. In very large amounts it can sometimes be used as an extra medicine to treat some cancers.

*   Smoking cigarettes, while harmful in many ways we can see, is also harmful to the body in ways we can't see. For example, smoking destroys vitamin C in the body.

*   Most plants and animals can actually make their own vitamin C. Humans, monkeys and guinea pigs are among the very few that have to eat foods with vitamin C, as they can't make their own.

OLIVER TWIST

LONDON
70
MILES

Oliver reached the end of the path and found himself on the main road again. It was eight o'clock now. He ran and hid behind the hedges until the afternoon, as he was afraid that he might be followed. He sat down to rest by the side of the road and began to think about where he should go.

The sign by which he was seated stated that it was seventy miles from that spot to London. The name created lots of ideas in the boy's mind. London! A wonderful place! Nobody, not even Mr. Bumble, could ever find him there! It was the very place for a homeless boy, who might suffer in the streets unless someone helped him. As these things passed through his thoughts, he jumped upon his feet and again walked forward.

Oliver thought about how he could reach his destination. He had only a crust of bread, a shirt and two pairs of socks in his bag. He had a penny too in his pocket. 'A clean shirt,' thought Oliver, 'is a very comfortable thing and so are two pairs of socks and a penny.' He changed his little bag over to the other shoulder and marched on.

Oliver walked twenty miles that day. All that time he tasted nothing but the crust of dry bread and a few sips of water. When the night came, he turned into a field and decided to stay there until morning. He felt frightened at first, for the wind moaned over the empty fields. He was cold and hungry and more alone than he had ever felt before. Being very tired from his walk, however, he soon fell asleep and forgot his troubles.

He felt cold when he got up next morning. He was so hungry that he exchanged his penny for a small loaf in the very first village through which he passed. He had walked no more than twelve miles, when night time came again. His feet were sore and his legs so weak that they trembled beneath him. Another night passed and the damp air made him worse.

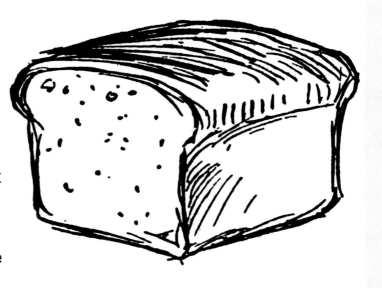

Seven days later, Oliver limped slowly into the little town of Barnet. The window-shutters were closed and the street was empty. Not a soul was awake. The sun was rising in all its beauty. Its light showed Oliver, sitting with sore feet and covered with dust, upon a door-step.

Suddenly, the shutters on the houses were opened, the window-blinds were drawn up and people began passing here and there. Some stopped to gaze at Oliver for a moment or two, or turned round to stare at him as they hurried by. However no-one helped him, or asked him how he came to be there. He had no heart to beg so there he sat.

He had been crouching on the step for some time when he was interrupted by a boy, who had passed him carelessly some minutes before. He had returned and was now looking at him most from the opposite side of the street. The boy crossed the street and walking close up to Oliver, said,

'Hello! What's the matter?'

The boy who was speaking was around Oliver's age but was one of the strangest boys that Oliver had even seen. He was short for his age and had little, sharp eyes and his hat was stuck on the top of his head. He wore a man's coat, which nearly reached to his heels.

'I am very hungry and tired,' replied Oliver. Tears were in his eyes as he spoke. 'I have walked a long way. I have been walking these seven days.'

'Come with me,' said the boy, as he walked towards the middle of the street. 'I'll help you'. Oliver stood up and slowly began to follow him.

National curriculum practice tests

Key Stage 1

Test 2

English reading

Paper 2: reading answer booklet

First name	
Middle name	
Last name	

Total Marks	/ 20

> ## Questions 1-7 are about
> ## *Vitamin C* (pages 104-105)

(page 104)

1 In which **two** food groups is vitamin C mainly found?

_____

1 mark

(page 104)

2 How often should you eat vitamin C?

Tick **one**.

once a week ☐

each day ☐

twice a week ☐

each month ☐

1 mark

(page 104)

3 What type of fruit is an orange described as?

_____

1 mark

(page 104)

4   Why can't our bodies hold onto vitamin C for very long?

_____

_____

◯

1 mark

(page 105)

5   How does vitamin C help your brain?

_____

_____

◯

1 mark

(page 105)

6   **Find** and **copy** the word(s) that means the same as
made by humans.

_____

◯

1 mark

(pages 104-105)

7 Tick **True** or **False** for each statement about Vitamin C.

Statement	True	False
Smoking destroys vitamin C.		
Vitamin C helps our teeth stay healthy.		
Vitamin C can only be found in oranges.		
Most plants cannot make their own vitamin C.		

2 marks

Questions 8-17 are about
Oliver Twist (pages 106-108)

(page 106)

8 Where was Oliver at the beginning of the story?

Tick **one**.

in a town ☐

on a road ☐

in a field ☐

on a bridge ☐

○
1 mark

(page 106)

9 How many more miles did Oliver have to go before he reached London?

_____

○
1 mark

(page 106)

10 At the beginning of the story, why did Oliver run and hide behind the hedges?

_____

_____

○
1 mark

(page 107)

11 Why did Oliver feel frightened in the field?

_____

_____

○ 1 mark

(page 107)

12 Look at the first paragraph on page 107.

How can you tell that Oliver did not drink a lot of water?

_____

_____

○ 2 marks

(page 107)

13 *he exchanged his penny for a loaf of bread*

What does the word *exchanged* mean?

Tick **one**.

to swap something ☐

to charge a high price ☐

to take greedily ☐

to keep safely ☐

○ 1 mark

(page 107)

14 What was the name of the town that Oliver reached after seven days?

_____

○
1 mark

(page 108)

15 How can you tell that Oliver was upset when he replied to the boy?

_____

_____

○
2 marks

(page 108)

16 Why do you think Oliver decided to follow the boy?

_____

_____

○
1 mark

17 Look at the whole story.   (pages 106-108)

Number the sentences 1 to 5 to show the order that they happen in the story.

The first one has been done for you.

Oliver bought a small loaf of bread.   ☐

A small boy speaks to Oliver.   ☐

Oliver saw a sign for London.   ☐

The window-shutters in the town opened.   ☐

Oliver ran and hid behind the hedges.   1

1 mark

Grammar, Punctuation & Spelling: Paper 1, Test 1

P. wait (no marks)

Award 1 mark for each correct spelling.

1. green *(S8)*; 2. catch *(S3)*; 3. hear *(S36)*; 4. watch *(S30)*; 5. jumper *(S6)*; 6. warm *(S32)*; 7. morning *(S8)*; 8. Their *(S36)*; 9. family *(S9)*; 10. bedroom *(S12)*; 11. giant *(S14)*; 12. dropped *(S26)*; 13. station *(S35)*; 14. happily *(S34)*; 15. towel *(S19)*; 16. complete *(S8)*; 17. replied *(S24)*; 18. hospital *(S20)*; 19. usual *(S33)*; 20. chimney *(S29)*

Grammar, Punctuation & Spelling: Paper 1, Test 2

P. bank (no marks)

Award 1 mark for each correct spelling.

1. sea *(S36)*; 2. race *(S15)*; 3. world *(S31)*; 4. always *(S27)*; 5. pencil *(S21)*; 6. middle *(S18)*; 7. Wednesday *(S13)*; 8. hopeless *(S34)*; 9. change *(S14)*; 10. knock *(S16)*; 11. July *(S22)*; 12. copies *(S23)*; 13. sister *(S8)*; 14. mouth *(S8)*; 15. fresher *(S7)*; 16. carries *(S23)*; 17. unnel *(S19)*; 18. patted *(S26)*; 19. scared *(S8)*; 20. alphabet *(S10)*

Grammar, Punctuation & Spelling: Paper 1, Test 3

P. well (no marks)

ward 1 mark for each correct spelling.

. won *(S36)*; 2. rocks *(S5)*; 3. sound *(S8)*; 4. careful *(S34)*; 5. written *(S17)*; 6. nicer *(S25)*; 7. nothing *(S)28*; 8. kit *(S11)*; 9. little *(S18)*; 10. valley *(S29)*; 11. bridge *(S14)*; 12. knee *(S16)*; 13. humming *(S26)*; 14. pedal *(S20)*; 15. wrap *(S17)*; 16. soil *(S8)*; 17. thief *(S8)*; 18. village *(S14)*; 19. capital *(S20)*; 20. dolphin *(S10)*

Grammar, Punctuation & Spelling: Paper 1, Test 4

P. have (no marks)

Award 1 mark for each correct spelling.

1. live *(S4)*; 2. worm *(S31)*; 3. summer *(S8)*; 4. brother *(S28)*; 5. walked *(S6)*; 6. wheel *(S10)*; 7. huge *(S14)*; 8. boxes *(S5)*; 9. city *(S15)*; 10. donkey *(S29)*; 11. think *(S2)*; 12. animal *(S20)*; 13. crying *(S24)*; 14. wrote *(S17)*; 15. tune *(S8)*; 16. blew *(S36)*; 17. treasure *(S33)*; 18. jacket *(S14)*; 19. rescue *(S8)*; 20. knight *(S36)*

Grammar, Punctuation & Spelling: Paper 2, Test 1

P. a. looking; b. bright (no marks)

1. shouted; sat *(G1.2) 1 mark*

2. How often do you go to the library? *(G5.3) 1 mark*

3. an adjective *(G1.3) 1 mark*

4. because *(G3.4) 1 mark*

5. unhappy *(G6.2) 1 mark*

6. lions; food; night *(G1.1) 1 mark*

7. commands *(G2.3) 1 mark*

8. Award 1 mark for a response that explains it is because they are names or they are proper nouns *(G5.1) 1 mark*

9. an exclamation *(G2.4) 1 mark*

10. or *(G3.3) 1 mark*

11. Ben slowly walked home. **(**Past Tense); Ben went into the shop. (Past Tense); Ben looks at the magazines. (Present Tense) *(G4.1d) 1 mark*

12. There are pens, pencils and rulers on the table. *(G5.5) 1 mark*

13. –en *(G6.3) 1 mark*

14. a statement *(G2.1) 1 mark*

15. were; caught *(G4.2) 1 mark*

16. Award 2 marks for an appropriate question using correct question syntax, with correct use of capital letter and question mark *(G2.2) 2 marks*

17. silently *(G1.6) 1 mark*

18. full stop *(G5.2) 1 mark*

19. Jack's apples were placed into the baskets. *(G5.8) 1 mark*

Grammar, Punctuation & Spelling: Paper 2, Test 2

P. a. Accept an appropriate word in the past tense; b. How old are you? (no marks)

1. My sister visited the library. *(G3.1) 1 mark*

2. fell; stopped *(G1.2) 1 mark*

3. school; Friday *(G1.1) 1 mark*

4. when *(G3.4) 1 mark*

5. Award 1 mark for a response that explains it is because they are names or they are proper nouns *(G5.1) 1 mark*

6. Lucy cleaned her bedroom yesterday. *(G2.1) 1 mark*

7. wouldn't *(G5.8) 1 mark*

8. Chop the carrots and onions carefully. *(G2.3) 1 mark*

9. Award 2 marks for an appropriate question using correct question syntax, with correct use of capital letter and question mark *(G2.2) 2 marks*

10. boxes; lessons; watches *(G6.3) 1 mark*

11. enjoyed; clapped *(G4.1a) 2 marks*

12. an adjective *(G1.3) 1 mark*

13. The book is over there. (Present Tense); The shelves are dusty. (Present Tense); I lifted the book off the shelf. (Past Tense); *(G4.1d) 1 mark*

14. James bought a coat and wore it to school. *(G4.2) 1 mark*

15. The bus will leave the station on Wednesday morning. James will collect you and your friend. *(G5.2) 1 mark*

16. For my breakfast I had juice, tea and a slice of toast. *(G5.5) 1 mark*

17. an adverb *(G1.6) 1 mark*

18. exclamation mark *(G5.4) 1 mark*

Grammar, Punctuation & Spelling: Paper 2, Test 3

P. a. helpful   *b.* chasing *(no marks)*

1. a command *(G2.3) 1 mark*

2. stood; looked *(G1.2) 1 mark*

3. –ly *(G6.3) 1 mark*

4. kindly *(G1.6) 1 mark*

5. if *(G3.4) 1 mark*

6. won't *(G5.8) 1 mark*

7. What is the capital of England? *(G5.3) 1 mark*

8. cousin; Lucy, Italy *(G1.1) 1 mark*

9. My favourite football team is called Norwich United. I go to see them play each Saturday with my dad. *(G5.2) 1 mark*

10. looked; saw *(G4.1a) 2 marks*

11. The rain fell heavily during the night. *(G2.1) 1 mark*

12. The pizza has mushrooms, onions and peppers. *(G5.5) 1 mark*

13. I went to my local park on Monday. (Past Tense); I watch the ducks on the pond. (Present Tense); I enjoy going to the park each day. (Present Tense); *(G4.1d) 1 mark*

14. an adjective *(G1.3) 1 mark*

15. Award 1 mark for a response that explains it is because they are names or they are proper nouns *(G5.1) 1 mark*

16. Jack ate his dinner and drank his glass of milk. *(G4.2) 1 mark*

17. I have: I've; let us: let's; she is: she's *(G5.8) 1 mark*

18. Award 2 marks for an appropriate question using correct question syntax, with correct use of capital letter and question mark *(G2.2) 2 marks*

Grammar, Punctuation & Spelling: Paper 2, Test 4

P. a. Where are you going? *b.* Accept an appropriate word in the past tense *(no marks)*

1. lake; mountain *(G1.1) 1 mark*

2. Close the door quietly. *(G2.3) 1 mark*

3. Award 1 mark for a response that explains it is because they are names or they are proper nouns *(G5.1) 1 mark*

4. jumped; crossed *(G1.2) 1 mark*

5. adjective *(G1.3) 1 mark*

6. My friend scored a goal. *(G3.1) 1 mark*

7. but *(G3.3) 1 mark*

8. How high is the mountain? *(G5.3) 1 mark*

9. Lucy cleaned the table and washed the dishes. *(G4.2) 1 mark*

10. an exclamation *(G2.4) 1 mark*

11. We saw ducks, rabbits and birds at the park. *(G5.5) 1 mark*

12. bravely *(G1.6) 1 mark*

13. The boy whistled loudly. (Past Tense); This chair is broken. (Present Tense); I washed the car today. (Past Tense); *(G4.1d) 1 mark*

14. that *(G3.4) 1 mark*

15. a statement *(G2.1) 1 mark*

16. full stop *(G5.2) 1 mark*

17. Award 2 marks for an appropriate question using correct question syntax, with correct use of capital letter and question mark *(G2.2) 2 marks*

18. echoes; pencils; potatoes *(G6.3) 1 mark*

19. he would: he'd; have not: haven't; you have: you've *(G5.8) 1 mark*

Reading: Paper 1, Test 1

P. a Winter *and* Summer; b yellow *(no marks)*

1. (a) birds (hopping on the tree); b) grown-up people's feet in the street *(1b) 1 mark*

2. The speaker wants to play instead of going to bed. *(1b) 1 mark*

3. clear; blue *(1a) 1 mark*

4. Accept any response which explains that it is different in Summer / the opposite way in Summer compared to Winter *(1a) 1 mark*

5. The reader *(1b) 1 mark*

6. Accept any response which explains that in Summer the days are longer / brighter than Winter so it seems like it is still daytime / early. *(1d) 1 mark*

P. To be a grown-up *(no marks)*

7. The warm sun; The fresh air *(1b) 1 mark*

8. Accept any response which explains that the Fir Tree did not like to hear what the children said about it/ it was unpleasant for the Fir Tree to hear the children's words about being little. *(1a) 1 mark*

9. Accept any response which explains that some of the largest trees were cut down. *(1b) 1 mark*

10. It is afraid. *(1a) 1 mark*

11. In spring *(1b) 1 mark*

12. Egypt *(1b) 1 mark*

13. Accept any response which explains that the Stork thought the trees had been made into wooden masts on the ships. *(1b) 1 mark*

14. youth *(1a) 1 mark*

15. It was sad to be cut down. *(1d) 1 mark*

16. wonderful *(1a) 1 mark*

17. picture-books and toys *(1b) 1 mark*

18. upright *(1a) 1 mark*

19. Accept any response which explains that the story states the moon shone therefore it was late. *1 mark (1d)*

20. happy *(1a) 1 mark*

Reading: Paper 1, Test 2

P. A star *(no marks)*

1. Towards the east *(1b) 1 mark*

2. one year *(1b) 1 mark*

3. about eight minutes *(1b) 1 mark*

4. 150 million km *(1b) 1 mark*

5. sunrise; sunset *(1b) 1 mark*

6. ultra-violet light *(1b) 1 mark*

7. There are more explosive solar storms. *(1b) 1 mark*

8. light; heat *(1b) 1 mark*

9. in his home *(1b) 1 mark*

10. Spring *(1b) 1 mark*

11. tired *(1d) 1 mark*

12. to move quickly *(1a) 1 mark*

13. steep; little *(1a) 1 mark*

14. pop *(1b) 1 mark*

15. Accept any two of the following words: scraped; scratched; scrabbled; scrooged. *(1a) 1 mark*

16. Accept any response which explains that the story states the Mole came out into sunlight therefore it was daytime. *(1d) 1 mark*

17. Accept any response which explains that the old rabbit wanted the Mole to stop walking / the old rabbit was trying to get the Mole's attention. *(1d) 1 mark*

18. Accept any response which explains that the old rabbit wanted payment (sixpence) from the Mole for passing by the private road *(1b) 1 mark*

19. vanished *(1a) 1 mark*

20. **1:** The Mole was spring-cleaning his home. **2:** The Mole made his way through the tunnel. **3:** The Mole sat on the grass in a meadow. **4.** An old rabbit asked the Mole to stop. *(1c) 1 mark*

Reading: Paper 2, Test 1

1. shape *(1b) 1 mark*

2. seven years *(1b) 1 mark*

3. strong; light *(1b) 1 mark*

4. about 206 bones *(1b) 1 mark*

5. happening all the time *(1a) 1 mark*

6. It supports the top of the body; It protects the spinal cord *(1b) 1 mark*

7. Red blood cells carry oxygen all over the body. *(1b) 1 mark*

8. The skull has two moving parts. (False); Bone marrow produces two million red blood cells every second. (True); An X-ray tells doctors where there is a broken bone. (True); The ribs give support to your lungs, heart and upper body muscles. (True) *(1b) 2 marks*

9. his godmother *(1b) 1 mark*

10. Accept any response which explains that it shows Prince Dolor is interested in the cloak / wants to learn more about the cloak *(1d) 1 mark*

11. Accept any two of the following responses: He did not want anyone to find it; He did not want anyone to laugh at it; He did not want anyone to laugh at his godmother. *(1b) 2 marks*

12. He thought most about his godmother when he wakened in the middle of the night. *(1b) 1 mark*

13. Prince Dolor forgot about his godmother. *(1a) 1 mark*

14. angry; disagreeable *(1a) 1 mark*

15. Accept any response which explains that Prince Dolor could not use his legs / his legs were weak *(1b) 1 mark*

16. tired *(1a) 1 mark*

17. Accept any response which explains that the story states the Prince lived in a deserted and lonely land. *(1a) 1 mark*

18. **1.** Prince Dolor's godmother gave him a cloak. **2.** Prince Dolor became very ill. **3.** Prince Dolor wished he could fly like a bird. **4.** Prince Dolor's godmother visited him again. *(1c) 1 mark*

Reading: Paper 2, Test 2

1. fruits and vegetables *(1b) 1 mark*

2. every day *(1b) 1 mark*

3. citrus fruit *(1b) 1 mark*

4. Accept any response which explains vitamin C dissolves in liquid therefore our bodies cannot hold onto the vitamin for very long. *(1b) 1 mark*

5. Accept any response which explains that vitamin C helps to make a special chemical that helps the brain to function. *(1b) 1 mark*

6. man-made *(1a) 1 mark*

7. Smoking destroys vitamin C. (True); Vitamin C helps our teeth stay healthy. (True); Vitamin C can only be found in oranges. (False); Most plants cannot make their own vitamin C. (False) *(1b) 2 marks*

8. on a road *(1b) 1 mark*

9. 70 miles *(1b) 1 mark*

10. Accept any response which explains that Oliver was afraid that he might be followed. *(1b) 1 mark*

11. Accept any response which explains that Oliver was afraid because the wind moaned over the empty fields. *(1b) 1 mark*

12. Accept any response which explains that the story states Oliver had only a few sips of water. *(1a) 2 marks*

13. to swap something *(1a) 1 mark*

14. Barnet *(1b) 1 mark*

15. Accept any response which explains that the story states Oliver had tears in his eyes which shows he was upset. *(1d) 2 marks*

16. Accept any response which explains any of the following: Oliver might have thought that the boy would help him; Oliver was lonely and did not know anyone else in the town; Oliver needed help from someone. *(1d) 1 mark*

17. **1.** Oliver ran and hid behind the hedges. **2.** Oliver saw a sign for London. **3.** Oliver bought a small loaf of bread. **4.** The window-shutters in the town opened. **5.** A small boy speaks to Oliver. *(1c) 1 mark*

Notes for spelling script:
Grammar, Punctuation & Spelling: Paper 1

The spelling test should take approximately **15 minutes** to complete (not strictly timed).

Please read out the instructions below.

Listen carefully to the instructions I am going to give you.

I am going to read 20 sentences to you. Each sentence has a word missing in your answer booklet. You should listen carefully to the missing word and fill this in, making sure you spell it correctly.

I will read the word, then the word within a sentence, then repeat the word.

Do you have any questions?

Once the pupils' questions have been answered, you should explain that before you start the actual test that you are going to give them a practice question. Use the instructions below for the practice question.

Practice question

Read the question to the pupils. (Below is an example).

*The word is **tree**.*

*There was a big **tree** in the garden.*

*The word is **tree**.*

Check that all pupils have understood that 'tree' should be written in the first blank space.

Explain that you will now read the rest of the sentences and the missing words.

Leave at least a 12-second gap between spellings.

The target words may be repeated if needed.

The 20 spellings should be read as follows:

1. Give the spelling number

2. Say: *The word is…*

3. Read the context sentence

4. Repeat: *The word is…*

You should take care not to overemphasise spelling when reading out the words.

Scaled Scores

Scaled scores are available via our website:
www.monstersats.co.uk/scaled-scores/

Our Lady of Lourdes Catholic Primary School
Wesley Road
Hillside
London
NW10 8PP
Tel: 020 8961 5037